D0590957

Just like my

Mother used

to Bake

Just like my *Mother used to Bake*

RYLAND
PETERS
& SMALL

LONDON NEW YORK

Senior designer Toni Kay

Senior editor Catherine Osborne

Picture research Emily Westlake

Production Gordana Simakovic

Art director Leslie Harrington

Publishing director Alison Starling

Notes

All spoon measurements are level unless otherwise specified.

All eggs are medium unless otherwise specified. Uncooked or partly cooked eggs should not be served to the very young, the very old, those with compromised immune systems or to pregnant women.

Ovens should be preheated to the specified temperature. If using a fan-assisted oven, cooking times should be reduced according to the manufacturer's instructions.

First published in the United Kingdom in 2008 by Ryland Peters & Small
20–21 Jockey's Fields
London WC1R 4BW
www.rylandpeters.com

Text copyright © Fiona Beckett, Susannah Blake, Maxine Clark, Linda Collister, Brian Glover, Clare Gordon-Smith, Rachael Anne Hill, Fran Warde and Ryland Peters & Small 2008 (*see* page 64 for details). Design and photography copyright © Ryland Peters & Small 2008

10 9 8 7 6 5 4 3 2 1

ISBN: 978-1-84597-599-9

A CIP catalogue record for this book is available from the British Library.

Printed and bound in China

Contents

Perfect Bakes

Who can resist the smell of a freshly baked apple pie pulled straight from the oven? When it comes to traditional bakes, mothers are the experts. Many of us will remember weekends spent in the kitchen helping cook batches of deliciously sweet cupcakes for friends and family. There's certainly nothing quite like a mother's guiding hand in the kitchen.

For those of you who long to recreate those bakes from childhood, the recipes in this book will have you whipping up irresistible chocolate chip cookies in no time. Why not make a batch for your mother, or bake with her just like old times? A celebration of mothers everywhere, *Just Like My Mother Used to Bake* is a delectable collection of home-made cakes, pies, tarts and biscuits.

Fruity Bakes

For the best pastry results, always use a metal pie dish: it will get hotter than ceramic and guarantees to cook the pastry until dry and crumbly rather than soggy.

Blackberry and apple pie

1 RECIPE SWEET SHORTCRUST PASTRY (*SEE* PAGE 62)

800 g cooking apples, such as Bramley, cored, peeled and sliced

400 g blackberries

100 g unrefined caster sugar

milk, for brushing

caster sugar, for sprinkling

custard, to serve

a metal pie dish, 25 cm diameter, lightly buttered

SERVES 6

Preheat the oven to 220°C (425°F) Gas 7. Remove 1 piece of chilled pastry from the refrigerator and roll out until just larger than the pie dish. Put the rolled pastry into the pie dish, pressing the base and rim gently to push out any air bubbles. Layer the apple slices, blackberries and sugar over the pastry, piling the fruit high, then brush milk over the pastry rim.

Roll out the remaining pastry to just bigger than the dish and drape it over the fruit, taking care not to stretch it. Trim the excess pastry away from the edge and then go around the rim of the pie, pinching the pastry together with your fingers to seal. Using a small, sharp knife, cut a vent in the middle of the pie to let the steam escape.

Brush the pastry all over with milk and sprinkle generously with sugar. Cook in the preheated oven for 30 minutes, then reduce to 180°C (350°F) Gas 4 and cook for another 30 minutes until golden. Serve hot with custard.

Mixed berry tartlets

These delightfully fruity tarts are perfect as little snacks or as a tangy treat — refreshing on the palate, they are sure to satisfy any sweet tooth.

To make the pastry, put the flours, butter and orange zest in a food processor and blend for 1–2 minutes until the mixture resembles breadcrumbs. With the machine running, gradually pour 3–4 tablespoons cold water through the feed tube until the mixture forms a ball. Transfer the dough to a lightly floured work surface and knead until it is smooth and pliable. Wrap and chill in the refrigerator for 30 minutes.

Preheat the oven to 200°C (400°F) Gas 6. Roll out the pastry thinly on a lightly floured work surface. Using the pastry cutter, cut out 12 rounds and line the bun tin with them. Prick the bases lightly with a fork, then put a small piece of crumpled foil in each one. Bake in the preheated oven for 12 minutes. Remove the foil and return the pastry cases to the oven for a further 3–5 minutes until the pastry is cooked. Remove from the oven and let cool before filling.

To make the filling, cut any large fruit in half. Put the crème fraîche and orange zest in a bowl and mix. Spoon it into the cold pastry cases and put the fruit on top. Dust with a little icing sugar and serve immediately.

PASTRY

100 g plain flour, plus extra for dusting

100 g wholemeal flour

100 g unsalted butter, chilled and cut into small pieces

1 tablespoon finely grated unwaxed orange zest

BERRY FILLING

450 g mixed summer berries, including blueberries, strawberries and raspberries, hulled

300 ml half-fat crème fraîche or natural yoghurt

1 tablespoon finely grated unwaxed orange zest

icing sugar, for dusting

a pastry cutter, 7.5 cm diameter

small bun tins

MAKES 12

This is a tart filled with an uncooked lemon curd and baked in the oven until just firm. A refreshingly decadent bake, ideal for a lazy summer afternoon sweet treat.

Classic lemon tart

1 RECIPE SWEET RICH SHORTCRUST PASTRY (*SEE* PAGE 56)

1 egg, beaten, to seal the pastry

crème fraîche, to serve (optional)

LEMON FILLING

6 large eggs

350 g caster sugar

finely grated zest and strained juice of 4 unwaxed lemons

125 g unsalted butter, melted

1 tablespoon crème fraîche (optional)

a loose-based fluted tart tin, 23 cm diameter

SERVES 8

Bring the pastry to room temperature. Preheat the oven to 190°C (375°F) Gas 5.

Roll out the pastry thinly on a lightly floured work surface, and use to line the tart tin. Chill or freeze for 15 minutes, then bake blind following the method given on page 61. Brush with the beaten egg, then bake again for 5–10 minutes until set and shiny – this will prevent the filling from making the pastry soggy.

Lower the oven to 150°C (300°F) Gas 2. To make the lemon filling, put the eggs, sugar, lemon zest and juice, and butter into a food processor and blend until smooth.

Set the baked tart shell on a baking sheet and pour in the filling. Bake in the oven for about 1 hour (it may need a little longer, depending on your oven) until just set. Remove from the oven and let cool completely before serving.

Serve at room temperature, with a spoonful of crème fraîche, if liked.

*This fruity treat is made all the more naughty with
the addition of whipping cream.*

Victoria sandwich
with strawberries and cream

Preheat the oven to 180°C (350°F) Gas 4.

Beat together the butter and caster sugar in a large bowl
until pale and fluffy. Beat in the eggs one at a time. Sift the
flour into the mixture and fold in until thoroughly combined.

Spoon the cake mixture into the prepared tins and
spread out evenly using the back of the spoon. Bake in
the preheated oven for 20–25 minutes until golden brown
and the sponge springs back when pressed gently with the
tips of your fingers. Turn out the cakes onto a wire rack,
gently peel off the lining paper and let cool completely.

Slice a thin sliver off the top of one of the cakes to
create a flat surface. Spread the strawberry jam over and
top with the strawberries. Whip the cream until it stands in
soft peaks, then spread it carefully over the strawberries.
Press the second cake gently onto the cream and dust with
icing sugar, then serve.

180 g butter, at room
temperature

180 g caster sugar

3 eggs

180 g self-raising flour

3½ tablespoons good-
quality strawberry jam

140 g strawberries, hulled
and halved or quartered,
depending on size

120 ml whipping cream

icing sugar, for dusting

**two 20-cm sandwich
tins, greased and
base-lined with
greaseproof paper**

SERVES 8

A tart that celebrates the perfect marriage of raspberries and cream. This is simplicity itself to make, but must be assembled at the last moment to keep the freshness and crispness of the pastry. Sweeten the cream with a little sieved home-made raspberry jam and add a dash of framboise (raspberry liqueur) if you have it.

Fresh raspberry tart

1 RECIPE PÂTE BRISÉE (*SEE* PAGE 58)

2–3 tablespoons home-made raspberry jam

600 ml double cream, or 300 ml double cream mixed with 300 ml crème fraîche

2 tablespoons framboise (optional)

750 g fresh raspberries

150 ml raspberry or redcurrant jelly (any berry jelly will do)

a loose-based fluted tart tin, 20.5 cm diameter

SERVES 6–8

Bring the pastry to room temperature. Preheat the oven to 200°C (400°F) Gas 6.

Roll out the pastry thinly on a lightly floured work surface, and use to line the tart tin. Prick the base, chill or freeze for 15 minutes, then bake blind following the method given on page 61. Leave to cool.

Press the raspberry jam through a sieve to remove the seeds, then put into a large bowl. Add the cream and framboise, if using. Whisk until thick and just holding peaks. Spoon into the tart case and level the surface. Cover with the raspberries, arranging a final neat layer on top.

Put the raspberry jelly into a small saucepan and warm it gently until liquid. Brush over the raspberries to glaze. Put into the refrigerator to chill and set for 10 minutes just before serving (no longer or it will go soggy).

Indulgent Treats

Some brownie enthusiasts believe that only cocoa should be used, not melted plain chocolate, as it gives a deeper, truly intense chocolate flavour.

Old-fashioned brownies

100 g walnut pieces

4 large eggs

300 g caster sugar

140 g unsalted butter, melted

½ teaspoon vanilla extract

140 g plain flour

75 g cocoa powder

a brownie tin, 20.5 x 25.5 cm, greased and base-lined with greaseproof paper

MAKES 16

Preheat the oven to 170°C (325°F) Gas 3. Put the walnut pieces in an ovenproof dish and lightly toast in the oven for about 10 minutes. Remove from the oven and leave to cool. Don't turn off the oven.

Meanwhile, break the eggs into a mixing bowl. Use a hand-held electric mixer to whisk until frothy, then whisk in the sugar. Whisk for a minute, then, still whisking constantly, add the melted butter in a steady stream. Whisk for a minute, then whisk in the vanilla. Sift the flour and cocoa into the bowl and stir in with a wooden spoon. When thoroughly combined, stir in the nuts. Transfer the mixture to the prepared tin and spread evenly.

Bake in the preheated oven for 25 minutes until a skewer inserted halfway between the sides and the centre comes out just clean. Remove the tin from the oven. Leave to cool before removing from the tin, then cut into 16 pieces. Store in an airtight container and eat within 5 days.

Coffee and walnut cake

This tea-time classic feels like a little piece of childhood – bringing back memories of afternoon visits from grandmas and great-aunts.

Preheat the oven to 180°C (350°F) Gas 4. Beat together the butter and sugar in a large bowl until pale and fluffy, then beat in the eggs one at a time. Sift the flour into the butter mixture and fold in, then fold in the nuts and dissolved coffee. Divide among the prepared sandwich tins and spread out evenly. Bake in the preheated oven for 20–25 minutes until golden and the sponge springs back when pressed gently with the tips of your fingers.

Turn the cakes out onto a wire rack, carefully peel off the lining paper and let cool completely.

To make the coffee frosting, warm the cream and coffee in a small saucepan, stirring until the coffee has dissolved. Pour into a bowl, add the butter and sift the icing sugar into the mixture. Beat together until smooth and creamy.

Slice a thin sliver off the top of one of the cakes to create a flat surface. Spread with slightly less than half of the coffee frosting, then place the second cake on top. Spread the remaining frosting on top and decorate with walnut halves, then serve.

180 g butter, at room temperature

180 g caster sugar

3 eggs

180 g self-raising flour

60 g walnut pieces

2 teaspoons instant coffee, dissolved in 1 tablespoon boiling water

walnut halves, to decorate

COFFEE FROSTING

2 tablespoons single cream

2 teaspoons instant coffee

90 g butter, at room temperature

180 g icing sugar

two 20-cm sandwich tins, greased and base-lined with greaseproof paper

SERVES 5–6

The lightest and airiest of all sponges, rolled with a filling of yoghurt and raspberries. Strawberries are a delicious alternative, if preferred.

Hazelnut roulade

6 eggs

175 g caster sugar, plus extra for sprinkling

50 g self-raising flour, sifted

75 g hazelnuts, toasted and finely ground

1 tablespoon unsalted butter, melted

icing sugar, for dusting

FILLING

200 ml Greek yoghurt

125 g raspberries

a 30 x 20 x 2.5-cm Swiss roll tin, greased and lined with greaseproof paper

SERVES 6–8

Preheat the oven to 200°C (400°F) Gas 6. Put the eggs and sugar in a bowl and, using a hand-held electric mixer, whisk until pale, thick and creamy. The mixture should leave a ribbon-like trail on the surface when lifted.

Using a large metal spoon, fold in the flour and hazelnuts. Drizzle the melted butter over the surface of the mixture, then fold it in carefully.

Pour the mixture into the prepared Swiss roll tin and level the surface. Bake in the preheated oven for 15–20 minutes until golden and the sponge springs back when lightly pressed with the tips of your fingers.

Remove from the oven and turn out onto greaseproof paper sprinkled with sugar. Peel off the lining paper and trim the edges of the roulade. Roll up the sponge from the short end with the paper inside. Let cool.

When ready to fill, gently unroll the sponge and remove the paper. Spread with a layer of yoghurt, add the raspberries and roll up as before. Dust with icing sugar, then serve.

An extra-special treat for chocaholics — made even more indulgent when served with lots of whipped cream and fresh cherries. Use good-quality chocolate for maximum flavour.

Chocolate truffle cake

Preheat the oven to 180°C (350°F) Gas 4.

Melt the chocolate in a heatproof bowl set over a saucepan of barely simmering water (don't let the bowl touch the water). When just melted, remove from the heat and stir in the cocoa. Mix well and let cool until lukewarm.

Using a hand-held electric mixer, whisk the eggs, sugar and cornflour until pale and doubled in volume. Using a large metal spoon, fold in the cooled chocolate, then the cream.

Pour the mixture into the prepared cake tin and bake in the preheated oven for about 1 hour or until a skewer inserted into the centre comes out clean.

Remove from the oven and run a sharp knife around the edge of the tin. Let cool in the tin (the cake will sink a little in the middle). Remove from the tin and dust with icing sugar. To serve, cut into slices and add fresh cream and cherries, if using.

225 g plain chocolate

25 g cocoa powder, sifted

4 eggs, lightly beaten

50 g icing sugar, sifted, plus extra for dusting

1 tablespoon cornflour

150 ml double cream, lightly whipped

TO SERVE

lightly whipped cream

fresh cherries, pitted (optional)

a springform cake tin, 20-cm diameter, greased and base-lined with greaseproof paper

SERVES 6–8

BASE

110 g digestive biscuits, crushed into fine crumbs

50 g butter

FIRST LAYER

two 200-g packs cream cheese

2 large eggs

100 g caster sugar

¼ teaspoon vanilla extract

SECOND LAYER

one 284-ml carton soured cream

150 ml Greek yoghurt

2½ tablespoons caster sugar

1 teaspoon vanilla extract

BLUEBERRY TOPPING

250 g blueberries

50–75 g caster sugar

1 teaspoon arrowroot

a loose-based or springform cake tin, 20 cm diameter

SERVES 8–10

This is a favourite cheesecake recipe, and goes down a treat after a light meal or as a naughty afternoon bite.

Blueberry cheesecake

Preheat the oven to 190°C (375°F) Gas 5. Gently melt the butter in a saucepan, let cool slightly and add the crushed biscuits. Press evenly into the base of the cake tin.

Beat the ingredients for the first layer together thoroughly, pour over the biscuit base and smooth the top. Place the tin on a baking sheet and bake in the oven for 20 minutes or until just set. Set aside for 20 minutes to firm up. Mix the ingredients for the second layer and spoon evenly over the first layer. Return to the oven for 10 minutes, then take out and let cool. Refrigerate for at least 6 hours or overnight.

For the topping, heat the sugar gently with 2 tablespoons water until it dissolves. Turn up the heat, add the blueberries, cover and cook for 5 minutes, shaking the pan occasionally, until the berries are soft. Take off the heat. Mix the arrowroot with 2 tablespoons water and tip into the blueberries. Stir over a gentle heat until the juice has thickened. Set aside to cool, then check for sweetness adding extra sugar to taste.

An hour before serving ease a knife down the side of the tin, then push up the base or release the clamp. Spoon the topping over the cheesecake and return to the fridge before serving.

Family Favourites

Sometimes it's the plain cakes that are the best. This one is wonderfully buttery and zesty and is delicious served simply — cut into elegant fingers or squares. To achieve a really crisp, sugary crust on top, combine the sugar and lemon juice at the last minute and pour straight over the cake before letting it cool.

Lemon drizzle cake

140 g butter, at room temperature

140 g caster sugar

2 large eggs

grated zest of
1 unwaxed lemon

140 g self-raising flour

LEMON TOPPING

4 tablespoons caster sugar

freshly squeezed juice of
1 lemon

a 20-cm loose-based square cake tin, lined with greaseproof paper

SERVES 8–10

Preheat the oven to 180°C (350°F) Gas 4. Beat together the butter and sugar in a bowl until pale and creamy. Beat in the eggs, one at a time, then stir in the lemon zest. Sift the flour into the mixture and fold in until well mixed. Tip the mixture into the prepared cake tin and spread out evenly.

Bake in the preheated oven for about 20 minutes until risen and golden and a skewer inserted in the centre comes out clean.

Transfer the cake tin to a wire rack and prick the top of the cake all over using the skewer. Dust with 1 tablespoon of the sugar for the topping.

Quickly combine the remaining sugar and lemon juice in a small bowl and immediately pour over the top of the cake. Let cool in the tin, then carefully unmould to serve.

One of the most popular after-dinner desserts, who could forget Key Lime Pie? Its tangy sweetness is refreshingly indulgent, and will take you back to lazy summer afternoons spent with friends and family.

Key lime pie

Roll out the pastry and use to line the tart tin. Bake blind (*see* page 60). Reduce the oven to 180°C (350°F) Gas 4.

To make the lime filling, put 1 whole egg and 3 egg yolks in a bowl and beat until blended. Whisk in the condensed milk and lime zest. Gradually whisk in the lime juice.

Put the remaining egg whites and cream of tartar in a separate, grease-free bowl and whisk until stiff but not dry. Beat 2 tablespoons of the egg white mixture into the egg yolk mixture, then fold in the remainder with a spatula. Spoon into the pastry case and bake in the preheated oven for 20 minutes or until risen and just firm in the centre. Remove from the oven and let cool in its tin on a wire rack. It will deflate as it cools.

When cool, make the topping. Put the cream and 2 tablespoons of the sugar in a bowl, whip until softly stiff, then spread over the lime filling. Toss the shreds of lime zest in the remaining sugar and use to decorate the tart. Serve cold but not chilled.

1 RECIPE SWEET TART PASTRY (*SEE* PAGE 60)

LIME FILLING

4 eggs, 3 of them separated

one 400-g tin sweetened condensed milk

2 tablespoons grated unwaxed lime zest

150 ml freshly squeezed lime juice (5–6 limes)

¼ teaspoon cream of tartar

CREAM TOPPING

250 ml whipping cream

3 tablespoons vanilla sugar

zest of 1 large unwaxed lime, pared into fine shreds

a tart tin, 23 cm diameter

SERVES 6–8

A scrumptious family treat — who doesn't remember enjoying a delicious slice of carrot cake as a child? A sprinkling of orange zest in this recipe adds a touch of tang to the sweet frosting.

Carrot cake

4 eggs, separated

240 g dark soft brown sugar

zest and freshly squeezed juice of 1 unwaxed orange

240 g ground walnuts

1 teaspoon ground cinnamon

250 g carrot, grated

100 g wholemeal flour

1 teaspoon baking powder

FROSTING

200 g cream cheese

100 g icing sugar

zest and freshly squeezed juice of 1 unwaxed small orange

a loose-based cake tin, 20 cm square, greased

SERVES 8–10

Preheat the oven to 180°C (350°F) Gas 4.

Put the egg yolks and sugar in a bowl and whisk until thick and creamy. Add all the remaining ingredients, except the egg white, and fold carefully until the mixture is smooth.

Whisk the egg whites until stiff, then fold into the cake mixture. Pour into the prepared cake tin and bake in the centre of the preheated oven for 1 hour. When done, let cool in the tin for 5 minutes, then turn out and cool completely on a wire rack.

To make the frosting, cream the cheese and icing sugar together. Add a little orange zest and juice to flavour. Spread over the top of the cold cake using a palette knife dipped in hot water. Sprinkle with the remaining orange zest before serving.

Pumpkin pie

Pumpkin Pie is traditionally served at Thanksgiving, but makes a great after-dinner dessert for all the family. Butternut squash purée makes an acceptable substitute if pumpkin is not available.

Preheat the oven to 160°C (325°F) Gas 3. Cut the pumpkin into large chunks and bake in the preheated oven for about 1 hour. Scrape the flesh from the skin and purée until smooth in a food processor.

Bring the pastry to room temperature. Roll out the pastry thinly on a lightly floured work surface, then use to line the tart tins. Trim and crimp or decorate the edges as you wish. Prick the bases all over with a fork, chill or freeze for 15 minutes, then bake blind (see page 61).

Lower the oven to 160°C (325°F) Gas 3.

Put all the filling ingredients into a food processor and blend until smooth. Pour into the pastry cases, set on a baking sheet and bake for about 1 hour or until just set. Remove from the oven and let stand for 10 minutes, then remove the tart tin and let cool for a few minutes. Serve warm or at room temperature, not chilled.

1 RECIPE AMERICAN PIE CRUST (*SEE* PAGE 61)

PUMPKIN FILLING

1 pumpkin or butternut squash

100 g light soft brown sugar

3 large eggs

200 ml evaporated milk

120 ml golden syrup

a good pinch of salt

1 teaspoon ground cinnamon

½ teaspoon mixed spice

1 teaspoon vanilla extract

2 tablespoons rum (optional)

2 tart tins or pie plates, 22 cm diameter

SERVES 12

1 RECIPE SWEET TART PASTRY (*SEE* PAGE 60)

LEMON FILLING

1 large egg and 3 large egg yolks

125 g caster sugar

finely grated zest and freshly squeezed juice of 2 large unwaxed lemons

125 g unsalted butter, melted and cooled

125 ml whipping cream

MERINGUE

3 large egg whites

¼ teaspoon cream of tartar

125 g caster sugar, plus 1 tablespoon for sprinkling

½ teaspoon finely grated unwaxed lemon zest

a loose-based tart tin, 20–23 cm diameter

SERVES 6–8

For some of us, one of our earliest cooking memories as a child must be making this classic dessert. The buttery, lemony filling for this pie is a delight, and the cloud of fluffy, crisp-crusted meringue is mandatory for any Lemon Meringue Pie worthy of the name.

Lemon meringue pie

Roll out the pastry and use to line the tart tin. Bake blind (*see* page 61). Lower the oven to 170°C (325°F) Gas 3.

To make the filling, put the egg, egg yolks and sugar in a bowl and beat until slightly thickened and a paler yellow. Beat in the lemon zest, butter, cream and finally the lemon juice. Pour the filling into the pastry case and bake in the preheated oven for 20–30 minutes until the filling is barely set in the centre. Do not let it overbake.

To make the meringue, put the egg whites and cream of tartar in a grease-free bowl and, using an electric whisk, whisk until frothy and forming stiff peaks. Whisk in half the sugar until the meringue is thick and glossy. Fold in the remaining sugar and the lemon zest using a metal spoon. Pile the meringue onto the tart, swirling and peaking as you go. Sprinkle with the 1 tablespoon sugar and return the tart to the oven for 30–35 minutes or until the meringue is browned and crisp on the outside. Serve just warm or cold.

Teatime

Traditionally served with clotted cream and rich, fruity jam, these scones are a must for the tea table. If you can't get hold of any clotted cream, use whipped cream.

Scones with clotted cream and strawberry jam

225 g self-raising flour

1 teaspoon baking powder

2 tablespoons caster sugar

50 g unsalted butter, chilled and diced

1 egg

75 ml milk

TO SERVE

clotted cream

good-quality strawberry jam

a 4- or 5-cm biscuit cutter

a baking sheet, greased

MAKES 10–12

Preheat the oven to 220°C (425°F) Gas 7. Put the flour, baking powder and sugar in a food processor and pulse to combine. Add the butter and process for about 20 seconds until the mixture resembles fine breadcrumbs. Transfer to a large bowl and make a well in the centre.

Beat together the egg and milk in another bowl, reserving 1 tablespoon of the mixture in a separate bowl. Pour most of the remaining liquid into the flour mixture and bring together into a soft dough using a fork. If there are still dry crumbs, add more of the liquid. Turn out onto a lightly floured surface and knead briefly until smooth. Gently roll out the dough to 2.5 cm thick and cut out rounds using the biscuit cutter, using the trimmings to make more scones.

Arrange the scones on the baking sheet, spacing them apart, and brush the tops with the reserved egg and milk mixture. Bake in the preheated oven for 8 minutes until risen and golden. Transfer to a wire rack to cool. Serve warm with the cream and strawberry jam.

Macaroons

Macaroons come in many varieties, and make an excellent teatime treat if you fancy something a little sweet. Crisp on the outside and chewy in the middle, these delicate fancies are perfect for balancing on the edge of your saucer.

Preheat the oven to 180°C (350°F) Gas 4. Scatter the pistachio nuts on the unlined baking sheet and bake in the preheated oven for about 3 minutes. Tip into a clean tea towel and rub together to remove the brown papery skins. Put the pistachios and icing sugar in a food processor and process until finely ground.

Put the egg whites in a clean bowl and whisk to form stiff peaks. Sprinkle the pistachio mixture over and gently fold into the mixture. Spoon into the piping bag and pipe 2-cm rounds onto the lined baking sheets, spacing them slightly apart. Bake in the preheated oven for 10–12 minutes until light golden. Let cool slightly, then carefully remove using a palette knife and transfer to a wire rack to cool completely.

To serve, stir the mascarpone into the chocolate until well blended, then use to sandwich the macaroons together.

115 g shelled pistachio nuts

115 g icing sugar

2 egg whites

1½ tablespoons mascarpone

15 g dark chocolate, melted and cooled

a piping bag fitted with a 1-cm round nozzle

3 baking sheets, 2 lined with greaseproof paper

MAKES ABOUT 16

Muffins are quick and easy to prepare and make a lovely brunch snack, especially when served warm with coffee. Blueberries make a delicious muffin, but you could replace them with raspberries if you prefer.

Warm blueberry and almond muffins

200 g plain flour

1½ teaspoons baking powder

1 teaspoon mixed spice

50 g ground almonds

175 g sugar

1 egg

300 ml buttermilk

50 g butter, melted

250 g blueberries

15 g almonds, chopped

a 12-hole muffin tin, lined with 10 paper muffin cases

MAKES 10

Preheat the oven to 200°C (400°F) Gas 6. Sift the flour, baking powder and mixed spice into a bowl and stir in the ground almonds and sugar. Put the egg, buttermilk and melted butter in a second bowl and beat well. Stir into the dry ingredients to make a smooth batter.

Fold in the blueberries, then spoon the mixture into the muffin cases filling them three-quarters full. Scatter with the chopped almonds and bake in the preheated oven for 18–20 minutes until risen and golden. Remove from the oven, let cool slightly on a wire rack and serve warm.

Walnut tart and fudge ice cream

This soft, sticky tart packed with walnuts is superb with the easy vanilla ice cream marbled with fudge toffee.

Bring the pastry to room temperature. Preheat the oven to 190°C (375°F) Gas 5. Roll out the pastry on a lightly floured work surface and use to line the tart tin. Prick the base, chill or freeze for 15 minutes, then bake blind following the method given on page 61. Cool. Lower the oven to 180°C (350°F) Gas 4.

To make the filling, put the butter and sugar into a bowl and cream until light and fluffy. Gradually beat in the eggs, one at a time. Beat the orange zest and juice into the butter and egg mixture. Heat the golden syrup in a small saucepan until runny, but not very hot. Stir into the butter mixture, then stir in the walnuts and salt. Pour into the pastry case and bake for 45 minutes until lightly browned and risen. The tart will sink a little on cooling.

While the tart is cooling, make the ice cream. Put the toffees and cream into a small saucepan and stir over medium heat to melt. Cool slightly and stir quickly into the ice cream so that it looks marbled. Put the ice cream back in the freezer until ready to serve. Serve the tart at room temperature with scoops of the fudge ice cream.

1 RECIPE SWEET RICH SHORTCRUST PASTRY (*SEE* PAGE 56)

WALNUT FILLING

125 g unsalted butter, softened

125 g light soft brown sugar

3 large eggs

grated zest and freshly squeezed juice of 1 small unwaxed orange

175 g golden syrup

225 g walnut pieces

a pinch of salt

QUICK FUDGE ICE CREAM

150 g chewy toffees (such as Werther's)

100 g double cream

1 tub (600 ml) best-quality vanilla ice cream, softened

a fluted tart tin, 23 cm diameter

SERVES 6

Ever popular and hard to beat, chocolate chip cookies have always been a childhood favourite. This classic recipe uses less sugar and more nuts. Use plain chocolate broken up into chunks or a bag of choc chips.

Classic choc chip cookies

175 g self-raising flour

a pinch of salt

a good pinch of bicarbonate of soda

115 g unsalted butter, very soft

60 g caster sugar

60 g light muscovado sugar

½ teaspoon vanilla extract

1 large egg, lightly beaten

175 g plain choc chunks or chips

75 g walnut or pecan pieces

several baking sheets, greased

MAKES 24

Preheat the oven to 190°C (375°F) Gas 5. Put all the ingredients in a large bowl and mix thoroughly with a wooden spoon.

Drop heaped teaspoons of the mixture onto the prepared sheets, spacing them well apart.

Bake in the preheated oven for 8–10 minutes until lightly coloured and just firm.

Let cool on the sheets for a minute, then transfer to a wire rack to cool completely.

Store in an airtight container and eat within 5 days or freeze for up to a month.

Sweet rich shortcrust pastry

This is a wonderfully light and crumbly pastry. It is best used for richer pies and tarts, or where the shell is more than just a carrier for the filling and the taste of the pastry is important. It can be made in a food processor, but the classic method gives a slightly lighter result – and besides, there is something satisfying about making pastry by hand.

USE FOR CLASSIC LEMON TART (PAGE 14) AND WALNUT TART (PAGE 53)

250 g plain flour

½ teaspoon salt

2 tablespoons icing sugar

125 g unsalted butter, chilled and diced

2 egg yolks

2 tablespoons iced water

MAKES ABOUT 400 G PASTRY, enough to line a tart tin, 23–25 cm diameter, or to make a double crust for a deep pie plate, 20–23 cm diameter

1 Sift the flour, salt and icing sugar together into a bowl, then rub in the butter.

2 Mix the egg yolks with the iced water. Add to the flour, mixing together lightly with a knife.
Note The pastry must have some water in it or it will be too difficult to handle. If it is still too dry, add a little more water, sprinkling it over the flour mixture 1 tablespoon at a time.

3 Turn the mixture out onto a lightly floured work surface.

4 Knead lightly with your hands until smooth.

5 Form the dough into a rough ball.

6 Flatten slightly, then wrap in clingfilm and chill for at least 30 minutes before rolling out.

Pâte brisée

This pastry is really the French version of an unsweetened shortcrust. It has a finer texture so should be rolled out much thinner – to about 3 mm. Sometimes unsweetened pâte brisée is used for fruit tarts that are baked for a long time, because other pastries with a high sugar content would scorch before the fruit was cooked. This pastry provides a firm, crisp support for the fruit. Don't be tempted to leave out the water – it makes the pastry stronger and easier to handle in the end.

USE FOR FRESH RASPBERRY TART (PAGE 18)

200 g plain flour

a large pinch of salt

100 g unsalted butter, diced, at room temperature

1 medium egg yolk

2½–3 tablespoons iced water

MAKES ABOUT 350 G PASTRY, enough to line a tart tin, 25 cm diameter or 6 tartlet tins, 9 cm diameter

1–2 Sift the flour and salt into a mound on a clean work surface. Make a well in the middle with your fist.

3 Put the butter and egg yolk into the well and using the fingers of one hand 'peck' the eggs and butter together until they resemble scrambled eggs.

4 Using a palette knife or pastry scraper, flick the flour over the egg mixture and chop through until almost amalgamated.

5 Sprinkle with the water and chop again.

6 Bring together quickly with your hands. Knead lightly into a ball, then flatten slightly. Wrap in clingfilm and chill for at least 30 minutes. Let it return to room temperature before rolling out.

Sweet tart pastry

This pastry is easily made in a food processor and creates a crisp, biscuity crust.

USE FOR KEY LIME PIE (PAGE 37) AND LEMON MERINGUE PIE (PAGE 42)

180 g plain flour

a pinch of salt

40 g icing sugar

100 g unsalted butter, chilled and diced

1 large egg, separated

1½–2 tablespoons cold lemon juice or iced water

a loose-based tart tin, 23–25 cm diameter, 2.5–5 cm deep

MAKES 1 TART CASE, enough to line a tart tin, 25 cm diameter

1 Put the flour, salt, sugar and butter in a food processor fitted with metal blades. Process until the ingredients are thoroughly mixed and the mixture has a sandy appearance. Add the egg yolk and 1½ tablespoons of the lemon juice and process again until the dough forms a ball and leaves the side of the bowl. Add extra lemon juice or water if the dough seems dry and crumbly.

2 Form the dough into a ball, pressing it gently to get rid of cracks, wrap in foil and chill for 1 hour. Remove from the refrigerator and let the pastry 'soften' for 10–15 minutes at room temperature before rolling out. Put the dough on a lightly floured work surface and roll it out fairly thinly. Use it to line the tart tin, making sure you ease the dough into the corners without stretching it. Trim off the excess pastry.

3 To blind bake the tart case, take long, thin strips of foil and fold them over the edge of the tart, to protect and support the sides of the pastry case. Prick the base of the tart all over with a fork. Chill for 30–40 minutes.

4 Bake the tart case in a preheated oven at 190°C (375°F) Gas 5 for 8–10 minutes until lightly coloured. Beat the egg white with a fork to break it up. Remove the foil strips and brush the inside of the tart case with egg white. Return to the oven for 8–10 minutes or until the pastry is golden and crisp. Let cool in the tin before unmoulding.

The quantity for this American pie crust is enough for two pies — so you can bake one and freeze the other.

1 Sift the flour and salt into a large bowl. Cut in the fat using 2 round-bladed knives or a pastry blender (or do this in a food processor).

2 Beat the egg in a separate bowl or jug. Stir in the vinegar or lemon juice, then add the water.

3 Pour the wet mixture into the dry mixture, then cut it in with the knives or pastry blender again. Bring the dough together quickly using your hands. Knead until smooth either in the bowl or on a floured work surface. Divide in 2 so it is easier to roll out later.

4 Shape the dough into a flattened ball, wrap in clingfilm, then chill for at least 30 minutes before rolling out.

Baking blind

Preheat the oven to 200°C (400°F) Gas 6. Line the pastry case with foil, then fill with beans. Set on a baking sheet and bake blind in the centre of the oven for 10–12 minutes. Remove the foil and the baking beans and return the pastry case to the oven for a further 5–7 minutes to dry out completely. To prevent pastry from becoming soggy from the filling, brush the blind-baked case with beaten egg. Bake again for 5–10 minutes until set and shiny. This will also seal any holes made when pricking before the blind baking.

American pie crust

USE FOR PUMPKIN PIE (PAGE 41)

375 g plain flour

a good pinch of salt

250 g white cooking fat, chilled

1 egg, beaten

1 tablespoon wine vinegar or lemon juice

4 tablespoons iced water

MAKES ABOUT 675 G PASTRY, enough for 2 deep tart shells, 24 cm diameter

Sweet shortcrust pastry

This sweet shortcrust pastry is ideal for fruit tarts. Its high sugar content means it can burn very easily, so use a timer.

1 Put the flour and butter into a food processor and process until the mixture looks like breadcrumbs. Add the sugar and process briefly.

2 With the machine running, gradually add 3 egg yolks until the mixture comes together to form a ball. (Add the extra egg yolk if it is too dry.)

3 Transfer the pastry to a lightly floured surface and knead very gently with your hands until smooth.

4 Divide in half, wrap each piece in clingfilm and chill for 40 minutes.

USE FOR BLACKBERRY AND APPLE PIE (PAGE 10)

350 g plain flour

200 g butter, cut into small pieces

80 g unrefined caster sugar

3–4 egg yolks

Index

Credits